Scientific Boxing
By a
Fistic Expert
(Louis Shomer)

BLOCKING
  LEFT TO JAW

BLOCKING
  LEFT TO BODY

DUCKING RT. HOOK,
LANDING RT. TO BODY

DUCKING LEFT JAB,
LEFT HOOK TO BODY

FOREWORD

Time was when the art and science of boxing was in the hands of a few low-brows, who, for the edification of a group of gentlemen of leisure in and about town, hauled and mauled each other without much science to the King's taste and to the profit and loss of the idle but sporty gentry.

A certain fame or, to be more exact, notoriety, was to be won and not long retained by the usually beer-barrel-shaped, and often beer-containing, virtuosi of the "squared-circle." Perhaps these "pot-belly" bruisers couldn't sign their names without making sweaty crosses, but they won a sort of left-handed recognition from the "bloods" that frequented the London "Pubs," who bet upon this or that besotted fighter as they would on a pair of game-cocks or on a horse race.

Just when the "game" became respectable and accepted by the better "clawsses" is somewhat shrouded in antiquity, or at least in the conflicting claims of historians who seldom studied history; However, we do know that, like industry generally, Boxing, or as we know it now—Prize fighting—began to perk up, grow up, demanded and obtained recognition only when it got "in the money." When the people realized that here was an infant industry that was becoming lusty, powerful and dividend producing, like any business, they sat up and began to take notice of it.

Naturally, the game ceased to be just a game; and the illegitimate infant, which had been kicked and buffeted by every Sheriff and "constable" of every country in the Union, and damned by every church society in the land, now felt itself entitled to the protection of the law. It lost its social stigma, became respectable and was taken up, coddled and cozened by all red-blooded people, who accorded it the respect it really deserved. A million-dollar gate is too big a "baby" to sneer at.

In the excitement of seeing, hearing and reading by motion picture and radio, of the championship prize fight; here in America, the general public has lost sight of the splendid power for good this manly sport of self-defence can really be. Of course, one mustn't look a gift horse in the mouth. If the interest evinced by the public in the large sums of money paid to the principals in a championship battle produces the lure which every get-rich quick venture naturally carries with it, yet it does cause every little Tom, Dick, Sammy and Angelo to aspire to a well-built figure, a clean life and wholesome thoughts.

There are few boys today who do not know from the stories of the lives of the best prize fighters, the reason for their rise to fame and fortune; the years of clean living; the rigid training: the sacrifice of indulgence and dissipation that preceded the nights of glory in the ring; nor of the rapid fall from grace of those who deserted the straight and narrow path that led them to the top.

Not every one of us can be a Dempsey; or a Barney Ross, a Gene Tunney or any one of the dozens of idols of the ring, but each of us may learn the delight of being able to defend himself against superior force; the joy of a healthy body and a clean mind by following some of the simple rules laid down for the fighters; the glow of satisfaction in being able to understand from first-hand knowledge what ring terms mean; and the pleasure that comes with the thought, "I'm not just a 'dub.' I'm not awkward. I'm not the laughing-stock of my crowd. I can take care of myself."

It is to that vast number of our youth who do not perhaps aspire to be prize-fighters. yet who respect and admire physical prowess, courage and manliness, that this little book is dedicated. May it hold a place near the well-thumbed volumes of real literature on their bookshelves. that it may do for the body what the Masters have done for the mind.

THE AUTHOR

TABLE OF CONTENTS

FOREWORD i
WHAT TO CONSIDER IN FISTICUFFS 1
MODERN PRIZE RING RULES 2
MARQUIS OF QUEENSBERRY RULES 3
TRAINING 4
THE WRIST POLE 6
THE WANDS 7
THE TREADMILL 8
PUNCHING THE BAG 9
THE HEAVY PUNCHING BAG 12
SHADOW BOXING 14
"ON YOUR BICYCLE" 15
DEVELOPING THE CHEST, SHOULDERS AND FOREARMS 16
SKIPPING THE ROPE 17
A FIGHTING DIET, MATCH TRAINING AND PREPARATION METHODS 19
    THE JAB 21
    THE UPRIGHT 22
    THE CROUCH 23
    THE HOOK 25
    THE UPPERCUT 28
    GOING INTO YOUR SHELL (COVERING IN ATTACK) 31
    FEINTING 34
    THE RIGHT CROSS 35
    ROLLING WITH THE PUNCH 39
    PASSING THE PUNCH 40
    DUCKING, BOBBING AND WEAVING 42
    LONDON PRIZE RING RULES 45
    CHRONOLOGICALLY SPEAKING 50

WHAT TO CONSIDER IN FISTICUFFS

In the glare of the calcium lights, through the stentorian voices of the announcers, in the introduction of the gods of the "Ring," in some of the glory blows of the principals, the play and interplay of movement and motion, what is lost sight of by the spectator is the months of preparation, the years of hardening, the heartaches and defeats of the gladiators, and their rise overwhelming odd; to victory and the plaudits of the crowd.

We shall try to analyze for our readers when, where, why and how these "heroes" got where they did; to show how bodily strength, ring cunning and stick-to-it-iveness won for these men who have dedicated themselves to the arduous life of a prize fighter, so that from their lives and example, we may, in a modest way, glean truths that will help us to round sharp corners off our own unpolished styles, improve our well-being and develop the latent courage that is in every man.

We shall give, briefly perhaps, the training regimen used by the best training camps, presided over by internationally known "trainers."

We shall delve somewhat into the diet that shears fat and "excess beef off soft human specimens and hardens muscles and sinew.

We shall endeavor to point out the blows, punches and stances that have won victory for some of the best-known fighters and shall, we hope with generous descriptions, diagrams and pictures, attempt to illustrate how to avoid blows and how to land them with the utmost effectiveness.

We shall try to acquaint our readers with the ring parlance, the weights that constitute the various classes of fighters and, from time to time, indicate the winners and titleholders in the different weights.

Thus by precept and practice we hope to be able to give a more or less comprehensive idea to the student or even the casual reader, what the art and science of self-defense really is and how beneficial it may become in the daily lives of anyone interested in it.

We trust we shall succeed in making this book simple, instructive and entertaining.

MODERN PRIZE RING RULES

Most of the rules used today are those telling fighter what not to do. In fact, since the weights and rules of procedure are simply a modification of the Marquis oi Queensberry Rules, the only ones we may be interested in are those which state what infraction constitutes a foul. In New York State today, fouls do not disqualify a fighter so that be loses the contest. They merely count as another point against him during a certain round, or in some instances where the foul is flagrant, the round during which such a foul has been suffered is lost to the guilty fighter.

Here are the rules against fouling:

1. Hitting an opponent below the belt.
2. Hitting an opponent when he is down; hitting him when he is getting up after he has been down.
3. Holding an opponent or purposely maintaining a clinch.
4. Hitting with the inside or butt of the hand, wrist or elbow.
5. Holding with one hand and hitting with the other.
6. "Flicking" or "slapping" with the open glove.
7. Wrestling or roughing on the ropes.
8. Falling down without being hit (taking a "flop").
9. Use of the kidney punch (punching purposely at that part of the body over the kidneys).
10. Use of the pivot blow or the rabbit punch.
11. Butting with the head or shoulders, or giving the "knee."
12. Using abusive or profane language (if the referee hears it).
13. Not obeying the referee after being warned.

MARQUIS OF QUEENSBERRY RULES

While still a bit archaic, these rules show the influence of experience and the evident effort to remove some of the brutality inherent in the old-time fights. Furthermore, although the rules were used by professional fighters throughout the world, they were intended for "gentlemen amateurs."

It is this word "amateur" that gave and has since been giving, the athletic world the well-known "pain in the neck." It was even then very loosely used and covered such broken-down derelicts of the ring that could hardly be classed as either gentlemen or amateurs.

Yet, for what the powers that be may make of it. here is the definition as the Marquis of Queensberry might have liked to have it:

An Amateur:

Any gentleman who has never competed in an open competition, or for public money, or for admission money, or with professionals for a prize, public money, or admission money. and who has never at any period of his life taught. pursued, or assisted in the pursuit of athletic exercises as a means of livelihood. The committee reserves the right of requiring a reference or of refusing an entry.

Certainly there could have been only one gentleman who might qualify under the above definition: FRANK MERRIWELL. And he didn't exist, except in the imagination of his creator.

Then, here goes for a brief resume of the Marquis of Queensberry Rules:

1. That the entries he drawn to contend by lots.
2. Heavyweights are over 158 lbs., middleweights not over 158 lbs.; lightweights not to exceed 140 lbs.
3. There are to be 3 judges appointed by the committee.
4. That the contest take place in a 24-foot ring.
5. No wrestling, roughing or hugging on the ropes be allowed.

6. Each "heat" consists of three rounds, with one-minute interval between each; the duration of each round to be at the discretion of the judges, but not more than five minutes.
7. Any contestant not coming up to time shall be deemed to have lost the contest.
8. No shoes or boots with spikes or sprigs be allowed.
9. Competitors must wear jerseys (this ls so that the tender sensibilities of the noble patrons might not be hurt).
10. Gloves to be provided by the club.
11. Cups to be boxed for once in each year; the winner to receive a silver medal (of course. side-bets—and all the contestants made them—would not destroy amateur standing, since, officially, the committee was not supposed to know anything about them. They couldn't—and do any betting themselves).

There were additional rules covering almost every conceivable situation, but they were not materially different from the London Prize Ring Rules and we thought best to omit non-essentials from this little volume.

TRAINING

How is a fighter made to tick? We all know that no boxer worth his salt will dream of walking into the ring without a training period, even if his manager would let him.

If his lungs are to stand the combined destroying power of the cigar-smoke-filled air of the indoor arena and the gruelling punishment of constant motion, the prize-fighter must develop a pair of bellows that inhale and expel air with ease.

If his legs are to be able to keep from growing weak round after round, to carry his torso forward and backward, to help him charge forward and support the weight of his body and flailing arms. or to dance nimbly away in the fifteenth as well as the first round, or to cushion the shock of a paralyzing blow that sends tremors to his knees. he must do something to strengthen his leg muscles.

If his arms are to take blow upon blow, as he uses them to deflect punches of his opponent or to guard a chin from shattering like glass, or if he wants them to inflict punishment without tearing his own sinew, he must season his biceps, harden his forearms, make them accustomed to lift, haul and push, train them so that they will be able to bear increasingly heavier and harder work, so that when he climbs into the ring, they will not bunch up on him like locked automobile brakes, but will function smoothly and effortlessly.

If his neck is to be the pillar which will support his head as it receives an unmerciful pounding, or if he wants it to be flexible so that. he can easily bend it to the right or left to avoid a blow without moving his entire body, he must practice the proper exercises that will unlimber neck muscles, that will broaden his neck and make it a column that will resist crashing blows directly upon it or to withstand the indirect concussion which follows a terrific right or left to the head.

If he does not desire to break a finger, thumb or knuckle of either hand, he must learn to direct his punches so that they land squarely upon some unexposed portion of his opponent's anatomy and. with sensible miserliness, husband his resources of his digits and fists so that no useless blow be landed.

Finally, if he is to breast the attack of abuse, skin-pricking barbs and foul epithets which the usually blood-thirsty and ungrateful galleries hurl at fighters whom these "fans" sometimes develop a hatred against, he must steel his mind to deflect them as easily as he avoids the blows of his opponent. In addition to his body perfection, he must learn timing, and his nerves must he rested and his mind divested of every other thought for the moment, except the job at hand of making the other fighter give up the battle. To do this he must live clean, eat regularly and properly, give up late hours. eschew the flowing bowl, forego what most of us consider the comfort of tobacco and while in training at least, the pleasant though weakening influence of the fair sex.

A world-famous trainer has worked out with great success a schedule of training, which includes exercises that take care of the physical side of the fighter's conditioning. He has collected some simple apparatus which he uses to put the boxer in trim.

Later in this chapter we will suggest a way to carry out our own training without recourse to the perhaps expensive, though simple, apparatus.

THE WRIST POLE

This trainer we speak of uses what we might call a wrist pole. It is made of wood and comes in three sections of varying circumferences, all of them attached to each other, so made that the contraption looks like a telescope pulled out its full length. It stands vertically, so that the narrowest portion is on the ground, the next wider portion above that, and the widest part at the top. It is set in a frame, so that the whole pole turns by a twisting movement of the hand around the cube of the pole. At the top is a round, wide horizontal ratchet wheel, grooved so that a cord or cable can be wound around it. This cord or cable is connected with a weight, which may be made heavier or lighter by removing or adding weights. and the cord or cable goes through a pulley.

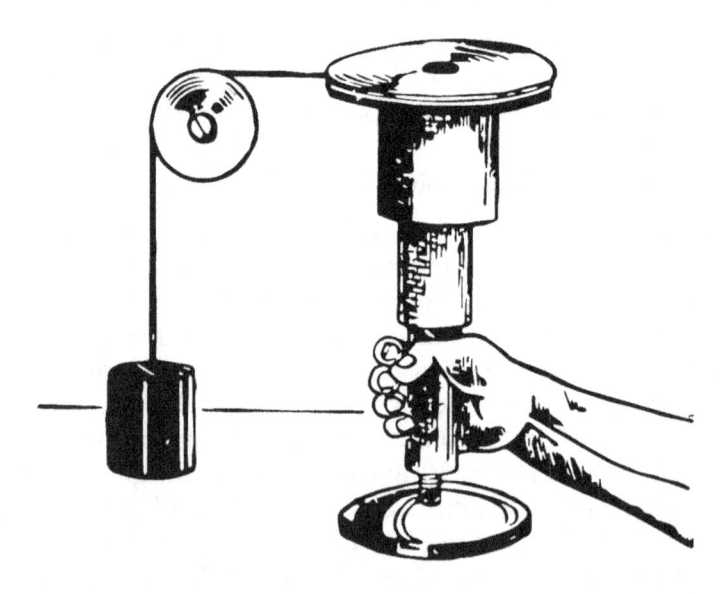

When the fighter grasps the section of the pole, the lowest or thinnest portion of it is just wide enough for his fingers to go entirely around it; the next width permits his fingers to go two-thirds around it, and the last and widest only half-way around it. By twisting the lower section, the pole rotates and pulls up the weights as far as the force of the twist permits it.

The whole idea behind it is to strengthen the fingers and the wrist muscles, As the wrist muscles become stronger the fighter will use the next section, oi which he can only grasp two-thirds of the circumference. This must cause him to exert more effort and puts a severer strain on the fingers and wrist muscles. Finally, when he attempts to twist the Inst section, if he is to have any success, his wrist will have become developed to the highest degree.

It can readily be seen that the forearm, too, will have received the benefit of this novel way to lift weights. The muscles of the forearm must necessarily expand with the constant strain of twisting. The human body is adaptable and nature will increase the size of the forearm and strengthen the tendons and the tissue if properly exercised in this manner. Thus, the fighter will be able to repel the shock which courses through his wrist and forearm when he connects with the body of his opponent. Without this exercise a torn tendon or broken wrist would be the price he would pay for his folly and might eventually destroy a career.

THE WANDS

The wands are hardly what one would call an apparatus and yet it is, taken collectively, when used properly, one of the most valuable bits of training "props" or the development of the muscles of the shoulder, arms, stomach and thighs.

They are, of course, as their names indicates, sticks, or light rods, each anywhere from three to four feet long. On the ends of each of the wands is a knob also made of wood. These knobs are used as handles, and the hands of both trainer and boxer are placed around these knobs and used in the following manner:

The boxer laces his right hand around the knob of the wand as though he were holding a door-knob and, holding it in front of him on a level with his chest, extends it so that the trainer grasps the other end in his left hand in the same manner. The trainer grasps a wand in his right hand around the knob and holds it extended out in front of him, shoulder level, and the boxer grasps the other end in his left hand.

The boxer will push the wand grasped in his right hand against the force opposed by the trainer, and the trainer will push the wand held in his right hand, while the boxer opposes the push with his left.

The boxer and trainer will see-saw back and forth, pushing the other back with one hand and resisting the pushing of the other with the other hand.

It can readily be seen that with two vigorous athletes straining to push each other off their feet, the muscles of the arm, the chest. the abdomen and the thighs come into constant play.

After a while the action will necessarily be slowed up due to the exhaustion of either one or the other. But a good trainer does not permit his man to do anything to the point of exhaustion. judiciously, he times the use of any apparatus so that every part of the body receives its measure of exercise without tiring. The trainer knows just how much punishment each muscle can absorb.

THE TREADMILL

Anyone who ever attended an old-time 'meller-drammer' of the Bertha-the-Sewing-Machine-Girl type is familiar with the treadmill. It is a moving platform or belt which works something like the tread of a cater filer tractor or "military tank" belt. The hero, heroine and the villain give the appearance of running by simply hopping up and down on the moving belt, although they actually do not move forward at all. This method is also used on the stage to show a horse race, where the horse or horses keep running on the treadmill ever onward and yet remain in the center of the stage.

The fighter in training may develop his leg muscles without leaving the gymnasium, if it is equipped with such a contraption as the Treadmill.

However, as few indoor gymnasiums can afford the rather expensive apparatus, and outdoor gyms seldom if ever have them, trainers substitute rope-skipping and road work with very beneficial results.

Along the by-ways of secluded summer or winter camps, one may often see a trainer and his boxer or boxers throwing up the dust or snow of the reads with aching feet. Often it is the fighter who calls quits and the trainer who punishes himself by running rather than permit his charges to find an excuse for stopping.

With head thrown back, chest out, arms held at the sides, fists bailed, the fighter either "treads the mill" or beats the road daily. This is almost a religious ceremony, so regularly is it observed, since wind, stamina, chest development, muscle forming, and fat removing are the result of faithful application to this form of exercise.

The fighter will dress up in a woolen suit, with an extra sweater or two, or a sweat shirt, and go through the exercise of running or hopping until his lungs breathe as regularly and as easily as that of a sleeping child's.

PUNCHING THE BAG

The amateur boxer cannot always obtain a sparring partner who knows anything about boxing or, if he does, one who is willing enough to be used as a dummy to experiment on. He either knows too much for our good, in which case it is human nature for him to hand us punishment that may discourage, even if it does not disfigure. Or, if he knows little or nothing, he may not relish being made an exhibition of and—retire with—a case of sulks or resort to brawling in which neither our science nor his ignorance will result in anything but a headache for both.

The light, fast punching bag is a sparring partner that receives for pay only a blow and, no matter how much punishment you give it, always comes back for more. It takes your hardest punch, but never returns it. Thus, whether you're a dub or a champ, it is the ideal sparring partner. It is justly popular with fighters of low or high degree.

PUNCHING THE BAG

No gym worth its name is without one or more light ching bags. But if you find such a place, desert the gym for a punching bag. It costs comparatively little and it is easy to find a spot in your home where you can attach it. If you had nothing else but this friend of the boxer, you could still learn a good deal about punching from this alone.

First of all, fix the cord so that the bottom of the bag is on a line with your chin. When you throw your arm and fist out to strike it, you will be compelled to hit straight from the shoulder. You will avoid the tendency to loop gout your blows. The difference between the scientific boxer and the gas-house rowdy is in the economy of motion which distinguishes the straight punch from the round-house swing.

You must practice straight hitting over and over until you have curbed the desire to leave go of a windmill loop that will probably do terrible damage to the ozone only. In boxing, too the shortest distance between two points is a straight line. Use only the straight-line blow, because it usually travels the shortest distance and is the most destructive.

Now, having learned to hit straight, you can raise or lower the bag so that you may judge the height of an opponent, if you ever get one to try it on.

Standing right in front of the bag, you strike the bag a little below the center with your clenched fist, avoiding any such fantastic formation of the knuckles as will permit one or more knuckles to protrude above the others. You hit the bag with that section of your fist that lies between your knuckles and second joints of the fingers. There's to be no twisting of the wrist or turning of the hand.

Having struck the bag, you drew your arm back its full length and wait for the return of the bag. After receiving the blow, the bag will shoot forward and up in an arc, hit the top-board, rebound and swing backward until it hits the top-board nearest you, then it will again rebound and when it reaches the point where you originally hit it, you will strike again.

After a while you will get the rhythm of the blow and the return and will be able to time your successive blows perfectly. At first slowly, then gradually increasing the tempo. you will continue to strike, withdraw your arm, wait for the rebound, wait out another rebound and strike in the same place and in the same manner. Eventually. as you speed up, it will begin to sound like a trip-hammer. Then it will become time to try the other hand, giving it the same workout. As simply as we can make it, this is how the action will look:

Sometimes, much to your disgust, you will find the bag seeming to have a mind of its own and instead of returning in a straight line, it will go off at a tangent. Don't work up any righteous indignation and begin wildly pummeling the innocent leather. It's probably either the fault of your imperfect timing or the intrusion of that looping tendency again. Just stop short,—and wait till the bag rests quietly once more. Then start punching again, slowly, carefully straight from the shoulder, gradually picking up speed, until once more you have it sounding like a riveting machine.

When it does, you will feel a justifiable glow of pride. Nothing inspires so much confidence as the ability to hit a bag regularly and gracefully. Should you, accidentally on purpose, take your light-o'-love into one of those penny arcades where they have a punching bag, you will surprise her with your masculine virility. She will undoubtedly fancy each blow as directed against some traducer of her maidenly modesty and clothe you with romantic knighthood.

Of course the practice is not confined to amateurs. The professional, no less than the casual boxer, uses the punching bag to improve his punches and has timing. It is as important as eating and sleeping to the boxer.

THE HEAVY PUNCHING BAG

This looks very much like a sailor's duffel bag, and is often stuffed with sawdust or some compound a little heavier. It is suspended in the same manner as the light punching bag, except that it has three cords at its upper end. Since it is not as resilient as the lighter bag, it does not swing back and forth as freely when struck.

It is this latter property, however, which makes it a necessity for the boxer. The greater resistance which he encounters in this large, heavy bag makes him expend greater force, and consequently develop a "wallop."

Our reader may find the purchase of such a bag beyond his means, and he may not have access to a gym which possesses one. This shouldn't cause him to abandon the use of it. It is comparatively simple to construct one out of a duffel bag, which may be purchased for little money in an Army and Navy outlet store.

To give it the proper body and some resilience, he may stuff it with sawdust and a judicious mixture of light sand.

One must, of course, be careful in punching such a homemade bag not to strike it with all the force he is capable of, or to twist or turn the fist when doing so, as it might easily result in a broken wrist or strained tendon.

Since the object is to develop a blow that travels a short distance and has the power of the shoulder and torso behind it, one should shoot his blows straight from the shoulder, moving the whole body with the blow. Do not attempt to strike from a distance, and do not hit it when it is swinging towards you. Below we give you a diagram of a heavy punching bag:

PUNCHING THE HEAVY BAG

SHADOW BOXING

When in some gym where boxers foregather you see a vacuous looking "gent" making terrific lunges into the air, than scowling fiercely and dancing around in the characteristic shuffle of a gentle elephant, don't take him for a punch-drunk "goof" or an escaped lunatic. Watch him carefully and you will see method in his madness. He is shadow boxing.

SHADOW BOXING

He is imagining an opponent, ducking his ghostly blows, blocking his lightning left or right and hunching his shoulder to protect his chin. At least, we imagine he is imagining. The boxer who does not have that ne plus ultra of the ring,—imagination—is and always will remain a "ham-and-egger." Those who have risen and stay there have the vision and intelligence that makes it possible to outbox and outfox an opponent.

The amateur may do well to follow his example. A light shirt and shorts, a pair of rubber-soled shoes, and he is all set. He thereupon pictures himself in the ring, facing another fighter who is skillful, tricky and dangerous. In this frame of mind, he will take a crouch or some other protective pose and proceed to defend himself, or to attack with the many blows we will set forth in later chapters.

One cannot overestimate the importance of shadow boxing. Not only does it improve timing, or the rhythm of punching, but it aids the feet in developing nimbleness and speed.

"ON YOUR BICYCLE"

In ring argot the above phrase usually means that some fighter has bitten off more than he can chew and is pedaling a figurative bicycle to escape the punishment his opponent wants to inflict—if he can catch or corner him.

In training, however, while this bicycle is still figurative, it merely means lying flat on your back with arms at your side, legs raised in the air, and being plunged up and down as if riding a bicycle.

This exercise is of immeasurable value for development of thigh and leg muscles, as well as the hardening of the abdomen muscles.

A few minutes of this exercise daily and you will feel an immediate improvement in your stomach muscles. It will serve to flatten the "bay window" you may be developing, and stretch the walls ol your stomach. A half hour every day and you will find yourself improving in every way, but by the time you are able to keep this exercise up for that length of time each day, you will notice the belt of fat around

your "corporation" disappearing and your abdomen able to withstand ordinary blows in that region. Do not, however, be rash and invite anyone to test the hardness of your abdomen by punching it at will. There are some who really can punch and, much as you may begin to believe otherwise, a stomach is hardly an irresistible body.

DEVELOPING THE CHEST, SHOULDERS AND FOREARMS

It is difficult to believe that any one exercise can do so much to develop the chest, shoulder and forearm muscles at one and the same time, yet, if you try it as we will attempt to describe it here, you will have to admit its almost magical qualities. Fighters in training follow it religiously.

Lie down on a mat flat on your back. Stretch out rigidly placing your arms by your sides. Then flatten. your palms down on the mat and raise your body on your hands, remembering to keep your heels on the ground. without shifting your body or head from anything but a horizontal position.

Keep on going up and down, trying to lower your body more slowly than you raised it.

Continue the exercise for as many times as you are able without tiring yourself too much.

At first you will be unable to do it for any length of time, but as you make it part of your daily body-building exercises, you will find your forearms strengthened, your shoulders learning to resist the strain and if you breathe deeply and slowly during the process, you will begin to feel your chest muscles expanding and gaining strength and power.

Even the neck muscles will come into play as you strain to keep your neck rigid and on a line with your body. The long, flexible muscles or tendons of the legs, the calves and thighs, will feel the energizing effect if the practice is regular and steady. Before you know it, you will be able to keep yourself aloft with ease, and the lowering of your body will be accomplished without unseemly haste.

Give a half hour a day to this best of all exercises, preferably in the morning before breakfast and the result will be beyond your loudest expectation.

Even if you never become a boxer, your whole body will gain a priceless healthy glow, a feeling of well-being will pervade every fibre of your body and you will be able to stand the strain of an enervating day with a cheerful smile.

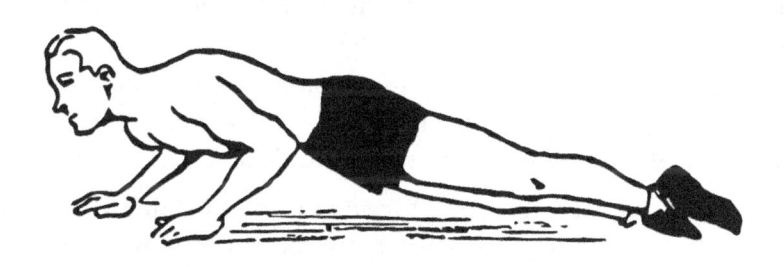

SKIPPING THE ROPE

The trainer may have a well-defined prejudice against having his boxer spend any time on the dance floor because, forsooth, the latter may learn to enjoy his dancing partner far better than he does his sparring partner,

But he is not at all averse to having his boxer dance, if it is done with a rope. Then, of course, he will call it "skipping the rope." In fact, he will urge it on him as one of the cardinal features of training.

He will tell him that he must do it if he desires to improve his footwork. Timing—of hand and foot—must be synchronized, and nothing will do that so well as the rhythmic skipping of the rope.

Is there any special kind of rope used? Well, it needn't be. But boxers do use a woven rope. at each end of which is a wooden handle. Your little sister has been using it on the sidewalks of New York or those of any other city. And yet there is nothing effeminate about the process. despite its humble origin. Only the fighter must do it with finesse. There's always a right and a wrong way of doing anything.

Start flat-footed. Throw the rope back of your shoulders. Then, when bringing the rope forward, rise on your toes and, as the rope strikes the floor in front of you, lift both feet slightly from the ground. The rope will pass under your feet and the rotary motion of your hands brings the rope up and over your head again so that you may repeat, slowly at first, the forward throw, the rising toes, lifting feet and the passing of the rope back again and over, ad infinitum.

Having developed a fine rhythmic movement up and down of both feet, you are now ready to vary the action and skip one foot at a time.

You place one foot in from of the ether, the heel of the forward foot being on the ground, while the toe of the other is directly behind it, the heel of that foot raised from the floor.

Now you turn the rope forward and, as it descends, you raise both feet of the ground. Continue this movement several times, then reverse the position of the feet so that the foot that was in front will now be behind the other.

After a while you will find that varying the position of the feet as often as you like will be as easy as it is to your little sister, with its beneficial effects being even greater for you. She will do it entirely for amusement—you for pleasure and business.

The leg muscles will become limber and supple, while your wrists. from constantly turning the rope in the snapping movement necessary, must develop a power that will aid you materially when you begin boxing.

A FIGHTING DIET, MATCH TRAINING AND PREPARATION METHODS

There is much the amateur can learn from the methods pursued by the professional trainer in conditioning a "pug" either for a debut or for another of his regular fights. It is, of course, plain that a difference exists between preparing for one's first fight or "keeping in trim" for one more. The fighter who makes his living with his fists must be in constant good condition. To him a break in training means a temporary let-out-of-pent-up spirits and an almost immediate return to rigid diet and exercise.

The occasional boxer, and the amateur, need not follow strictly any such Spartan conduct. All he has to do is to make for himself a set of rules that he will observe daily, departing therefrom once in a while, reasonably and without excessive indulgence.

But let us see what the professional does and then take from him what we can, bearing in mind the difference in our understanding and our objective.

First of all, the prize-fighter commencing training cleans his digestive system of all impurities; takes a good thorough-going but not drastic cathartic.

Then he starts the regular flushing of his stomach and kidneys by drinking of quantities of water; he does not wait until he is thirsty, but at set intervals and in amounts that at regular and will not bloat him. The tiny pores that cover our entire bodies ooze out globules of honest sweat when we exercise. This perspiration, of course, is a dilution of toxins, or poisons generated by our digestive tracts with water we drink. Thus, the greater the amount we drink the more we perspire and the more easily are the toxins eliminated in this manner. Along with the surface excretion by our pores, is the regular elimination of unused and unwanted waste matter through the intestinal tract. which, too, is aided by the drinking of copious drafts of water.

The body heat generated by vigorous exercises acts as a sort of animated frying pan, frying out every ounce of excess fatty tissue; then it is carried off in the streams of water we imbibe.

Then follows a diet so designed that it gives the fighter every type of energy-producing food to act as fuel for a smooth working dynamo, leaving out no essential carbohydrates, or hydrocarbons, and careful to exclude fat forming starches or sugars. Certainly not the type of diet so beloved of milady of today to give her that slender, sylph-like figure, but which also produces that drawn haggard, dissipated look and the scrawny. unlovely neck. No crazy eight- or eighteen-day diets to starve and shrink the stomach and to eat away necessary tissue.

The fighter does not miss any life-giving substance such as contained in red meats, cereals, fish and the vegetable greens that produce iron, calcium and essential salts. However, every dish is made with care, the quantities scientifically apportioned; no greasy, fried messes, no excess butter fats, and no such reasoning as makes the mouth of an epicure water and gourmet drool. For, if, as some great General said, an army fights on its stomach, the boxer not only fights but win; because of his stomach. A gastric disturbance in the midst of a prize fight would be a tragedy that might blast a career. The trainer leaves as little to chance as possible. Not all the fighting is done in the ring and skill without perfectly functioning organs is like a Rolls-Royce body covering an engine assembled from a junk-shop.

To the diet, the trainer adds rigorous exercise in and out of the gym—walks, and trots and runs, paced and un-paced; regular sparring bouts, shadow boxing, bag punching, rope-skipping; then invigorating cold and sometimes needle showers, and kink removing massages. No training camp is without its expert "rubber," the person who seems to ferret out every tight spot in every muscle. The fighter, on the night of his engagement in battle, is to be no such muscle-bound simian as you may see on the luridly illustrated physical culture periodicals. His muscles are limber and loose, with every tiredness ironed out, so that the public sees a clean-cut, healthy-skinned, springy, elastic-stepping youngster, filled with the joy of life.

Training camps have regular visitors who actually pay to see the fighter perform his daily stint, but there is one visitor that is neither invited nor tolerated: John Barleycorn. Why trainers, who themselves are not teetotalers, are so dead set against any alcoholic beverage for their fighters, is simple of explanation. "Booze," even in small quantities, tends to paralyze some nerve center; slows up the perfect coordination of mind and muscle that makes up the good fighter, and there is something in the very act of taking liquor that seems to break down discipline. The man who cannot govern himself from indulgence is hardly one who cares enough about his future to fight for it.

Smoking, too, takes its toll--shortening wind and saturating the body with a nerve-shaking narcotic. It is not here contended that all use of tobacco must be abandoned in order to be able to defend himself, but it is nevertheless true that, for the fighter or the man who wants to be a good boxer, it is well to do nothing that might weaken, in any way, any part of the body.

Lastly, during training the camp is an Eveless paradise. This is no reflection on womanhood. At home and surrounded by the things that make the home, woman may be God's gift to men, but out here where men are men and women are dangerous, the trainer, if he is given a free hand, will exclude the feminizing influence as though it were a blight. There are any number of fighters who have trained in night clubs, but if they are still alive, are now on the relief rolls or standing in some public places with a handful of pencils and shoe-laces.

THE JAB

There are few fighters who "pack" a knockout punch. For the most part, with the exception of those "naturals," or born fighters, contests are won or lost by outpointing a rival. It is therefore most important to develop the ability to reach an opponent often. Even a light tap counts for something when the judges mark their cards, preparatory to rendering a decision. The man who can beat a tattoo on another's face or body stands a good chance of winning, unless in the meantime he has been hit by one of those windmill "haymakers," which are potent even if accidental. True, it is to guard against just such an occurrence that boxers are trained and that books on boxing are written. Science should be and usually is superior to chance.

And yet, in passing we might note that in at least one instance a champion had been crowned who had been receiving a terrific beating and was all but out when, from some source, unknown (even to himself), he uncorked at swing that started at his bootstrings and landed by mere accident on the reigning dictator's jaw, knocking him from under his title and almost into oblivion. Well, the new champion lasted until his next fight. His manager knew he had won by a fluke and tried to capitalize the title into a fortune by keeping his fighter away from every lusty contender, but finally fate caught up with him. He had to fight some time and, when he did, he very ungracefully abdicated his throne.

But ordinarily, it is the humble "jab" that is the mainstay of the boxer, and by that we mean the man who depends on his skill in outmaneuvering his opponent rather than by "taking it" until he can land one lethal blow.

If you study the motion pictures after some famous fight, or if you look at the "stills" and poses of fighters in any magazine or sport-page devoted to boxing, you will note that almost invariably the stance or posture first assumed is either one or the other of two types:

THE UPRIGHT

From the upright position on his toes; his right elbow crooked where the boxer stands upright facing his opponent, one foot forward flat on the ground, the other slightly behind and to one side on his toes; his right elbow crooked, his gloved fist held close to his chest a little above the waist line; while the left arm is extended in front of him, not straight out and rigid, but bent at the elbow.

THE CROUCH

From the Crouch Position where the boxer faces the other contender, his body slightly bent forward, left foot in front of him firmly on the ground (both heel and toe), his right foot behind the other, on his toes, the knees slightly bent; while his right hand is held close to his chest, his right shoulder raised higher than the left (to protect his chin), and the left arm is held out in front of him, a bit crooked at the elbow, ready for either a jab or a hook.

CROUCH

From either one of the foregoing positions the boxer usually leads with his left and uses the jab, which is a sort of exploratory feeler. He lashes his left arm out, having taken aim for some part of the other's face.

The jab is nearly always an overhead thrust; that is, while it is straight from the shoulder and does not twist or hook, it is nevertheless something similar to the overhand stroke in swimming. It is done with the back of the fist facing upward.

The right arm, of course, is not a fixture. It is held against the chest to protect the vulnerable portions of the body; but when the left is jabbed in the other's face, he is liable to try a counter-attack, and here the right hand is used, being brought forward slightly to catch the blow before it succeeds in landing on the face or body.

Both actions,—the left jab and the right block—are accomplished also by using a slight body sway, first towards the right with the left hip, and then to the left with the right hip; the complete action being carried out as if it were one movement. Constant practice will make this movement instinctive. One has no time to deliberate in the ring.

The hip-sway with the left jab adds the weight of the body to the thrust of the arm and lends strength to the blow, so that instead of being just a tap, it may often do real damage.

It is not unusual to see a seasoned fighter use the left jab continuously. Joe Louis, The Sepia Cyclone from Detroit, inflicted severe punishment on those who ventured into the ring with him by constantly flicking that long straight left of his in their faces just as they got themselves set for what might have been sleeping potions if they had landed. Those tantalizing left jabs peppering their proboscis, often tilting their heads backward, began to develop inferiority complexes in his opponents. It softened their desire to rush him and kept them at respectful distances away from him, so that his longer reach and panther-like agility began to take toll of their strength and willpower.

Not every jab lands. It often happens that the object of your jabs anticipates your moves, and either moves his head to the right or left to avoid them, or ducks under your extended arm. If you just jabbed with your left hand and forgot all about the right, you might readily have a rendezvous with a doctor, for your opponent jab on you and he will aim for that part of your body which you left unprotected. One must never drop the right arm from its position in front of his chest, but use it to ward of blows aimed for the midriff or head by lowering it slightly to contact the oncoming blow or raising it to cover the chest and chin, or again to push aside a well-directed left or right. The left jab is your firs line of offense and the right the first and last row of defense.

Lastly, remember that, to have any effect, the jab must have the weight of your body behind it. Consequently, you must jab, when you do, while you are moving forward. It is evident that if you are hacking away to evade a blow, the extension of your left arm, in an effort to jab the other, will have no value, even if you land, for at best it can only be a glancing blow. There is no accurate aim and but little purpose.

THE HOOK

It is said of Jack Dempsey, who has become almost a legend in the ring, that. the amazing thing about his style of fighting was the elimination of waste motion. Such was the coldness and ring generalship with which he fought, that every blow was thought out and planned so that the moment the opportunity presented itself he was in with the ferocity of a tiger, the strength of a lion, and the guile of a fox.

His blows, some have said, traveled only a few inches at times and at most a few feet. From this it is evident that most of his damaging blows were "hooks" with plenty of steam on them.

What is a hook?

Well, in the first place it isn't a jab, which means that it's never an overhand blow.

Secondly, it isn't a swing. That, of course, presupposes that it must be a short blow. And that's exactly what it is.

It is executed in this manner:

You spar off facing your opponent in the usual manner, either standing up or in a crouch, one arm extended slightly, the other held closely to your chest.

Your opponent leads with his left in a jab—the feeler most people will start with. You sidestep, not to your right, away from him, but to your left, so that his blow will pass harmlessly over your right shoulder.

25

His left fist is now useless to him, so he will have to use his other hand. He'll bring up his right intending to hit you with it. Your first reaction would be to step away from it. That would indeed be poor boxing, for, while you would be escaping possible punishment, you would also leave him in possession of the field.

No, you must step in. You are now close to him. His left arm is over your right shoulder. The left side of his body is now unprotected.

You bring your right arm up in a short, round loop, an arc in which your fist is higher than your elbow, and in which your fist strikes his body in such a way that the knuckles face the body and come in contact with his stomach at a sort of angle. However, the striking surface of your fist is that portion of it which is between the knuckles and the first joints of your fingers.

RIGHT HOOK TO BODY

(a) Left Hook. Of course, the left hook is executed in the same manner as the right, except with the left fist, and where the action of your opponent is reversed.

What makes the hook so damaging is the fact that most fighters add to the force of that short, ugly blow the weight of their body, by lifting the right leg off its heel and twisting the hip in the direction of the blow. Thus your opponent lets not only the concussion of the fist against his unprotected stomach, but the additional power of the swinging hip and right side of the body.

LEFT HOOK TO FACE

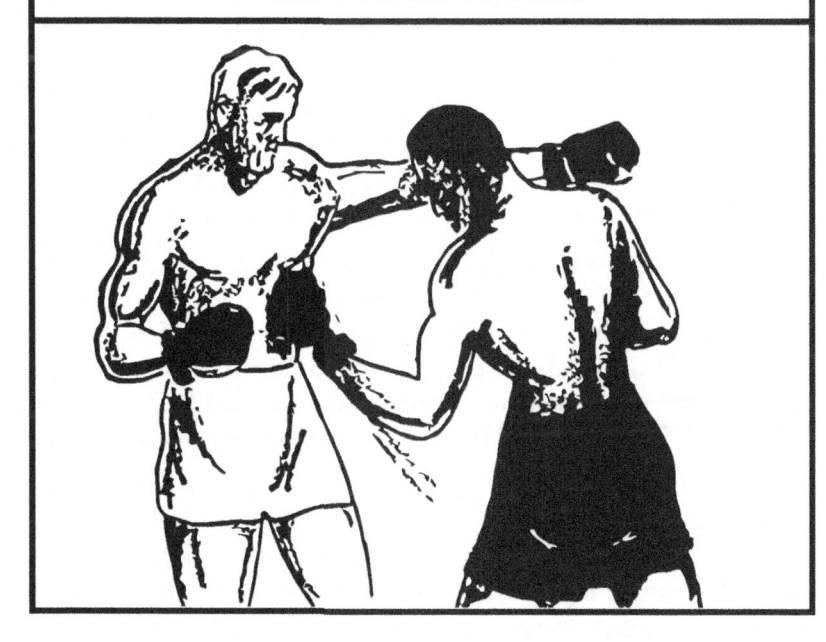

THE UPPERCUT

The lay public. and by that we mean, among others, those who see a fight only once in a while and who can take it or leave it alone, generally regard the ring "greats" with tongue in cheek and a sneaking leer that harbors on contempt for the note of reverence that appears in the mention of certain of the prize-fight immortals. That, of course, argues either ignorance or indifference.

There are, however, names in Fistiana that justly wear an aura. Their halo comes from an honest appreciation of the science of fisticuffs and from the determination to hear the injunction of that other robust American, Theodora "Roosevelt, "When you play, play hard and when you work, work hard."

No other man so typifies, in the ring at least, that spirit of "giving value received" as Terry McGovern. In a day when great fighters were the rule rather than the exception, he stood out like a shining light in a murky world.

"Terrible Terry" was what they called him. Out of the ring the softest spoken of men, he was a holy terror in it. His square, pugnacious jaw, the feral glitter in his eyes, his animal crouch struck terror into the heart of an opponent and his lusty Fists completed the demoralization.

He was what we now know as a great "in-fighter." He wasted no effort in lunging swings that (but for the grace of the other's knowledge) might assassinate. He did his greatest damage when he closed in on his man—,and he always closed in on him.

His most devastating blow was the "Upper-cut." It would be too much to say that he was the inventor or even the discoverer of this lethal weapon, but it would not be exaggerating to say that he was the greatest of all its exponents and that our modem fighters have had his use of it dinned into their ears by trainers who saw him annihilate fighters with it.

To say that the blow itself is simple would hardly seem to merit the long introduction. But every blow, when analyzed, is simple and, since knowledge generally is cumulative, it can readily be seen that it is the accumulated knowledge of many simple blows and their use whenever the opportunity presents itself that bespeaks success in the ring.

Very much like the hook is the uppercut. In that it should not, even if it could, be used at long range.

Imagine again that you are standing toe to toe with your opponent. He reaches over with a long, overhand left. This is either just a swing, or it is a jab. In either case, you now know that you must evade it somehow and that the best and easiest way to do it is to side-step or duck.

If you step to the left of his blow just a little, the blow will pass over your right shoulder. That leaves his whole left side exposed. He is open for one of two blows—if you step in. You may give him the body-blow we described in the previous chapter—the hook, or you can try the uppercut.

You throw your arm—your right, since it is that arm that faces his exposed right side—UPWARD, with your gloved fingers facing your own body. It travels only a short distance, as you have stepped in until you are very close to him.

It moves in an underhand arc, sort of sliding along the length of his stomach until it strikes his chin. Because your fist is clenched and the fingers facing your own body, it is the knuckles of your fist that contact his chin.

The slight twist that you gave your right hip, as in the hook, tends to add force to your blow.

His chin will snap upward, his head backward. Often such a blow will send his body back on its heels and, if the blow is unexpected and the fighter is not set for it, he will be thrown violently to the ground.

Let us see if we cannot describe it in pictures.

Practice this blow over and over again. It will prove invaluable.

Remember, whether your opponent throws or swings his left or right overhand toward you, do not step away backward. His reach may be longer than you think. He may still connect. Your only defense is to side-step. If it is his right hand, you sidestep to his left, if it is his left hand, step to his right. Then close in and under his extended arm. Keep your arm bent at the elbow directly in front of you so that the inside of the forearm faces upward, the palm of your hand facing your own body; the knuckles of your hand also facing upward. You do not swing your blow. You lift your arm, aided by your hip-twist, with force until it strikes his chin or under it.

During all this time your free arm is held close to your own chest so that you may be covered in case he should recover from his unsuccessful lunge or should attempt to bring his other hand into play. You may either catch his other glove on your hand or push it aside.

SPARRING OFF

LEFT JAB AND PASSING PUNCH

CLOSING IN

RIGHT UPPER-CUT- AND OUT!

JAB SHORT

BLOCKING JAB

RT. HOOK TO JAW

-AND OUT!

GOING INTO YOUR SHELL (COVERING IN ATTACK)

"Flash-in-the-pans" come and go across the fistic horizon like shooting-stars. They have their own brief moment of glory, radiate a glow, let off a few celestial fireworks, and then fall to earth and darkness, unsung and forgotten.

The fans love these meteoric careers while they are still emitting sparks, but the fighter of intelligence and,—despite reports to the contrary, there are some—knows that to survive in this most competitive sport he must conserve his energies, husband his resources of strength and skill and take as little punishment as possible.

That doesn't mean that he must be cautious to the point of cowardice. Woe unto the fighter that goes into-battle with the thought of keeping his features regular and his hair parted neatly in the center. He is a sucker for the rough, tough, one-track minded youngster who carries mayhem in each feet and murder in his heart.

Yet, "he who fights and runs away will live to fight another day." So, despite a few unsympathetic jeers, the clever boxer "goes into his shell" when the going is bad. But even here he does it with malice aforethought. His outlook is to protect himself but to hold his powder until he "sees the whites" of the other's eyes, then let fly.

Tony Canzoneri, that perennial champion of light-weights, that constant thrill-monger, who is a delight to the eye, is not averse to "covering up" if need be. He is known as the man who never steps back. He will be found wading in and flailing away at the last bell as lustily as he was at the first.

But it isn't necessary to "go into your shell' by running away from punishment.

When the fighter finds himself suddenly confronted by a barrage of blows--lefts, rights, one-two's, and a few others he never heard of and he has had no time to set himself either for a defense or offense, he must "cover-up." That means that he will fall into a crouch, so that his chin sinks into his chest like the neck of a turtle, his right shoulder will hunch up higher than his left, and his arms will be extended around and in front of his face, somewhat like a cross. His elbows will jut out from the sides of his body, his wrists will cover his face, and the gloves protect him from attack on the head.

But this is temporary—and the criss-cross placement of his arms is not rigid. The arms are held crossed in front loosely and in such a manner that either the left or right may be withdrawn any time with as little commotion as possible, cocked, and let fly when the other is complimenting himself on doing severe damage.

It is just at the point when your opponent is throwing his lefts and rights that the crouch and the ducking, the bobbing and weaving, which merely means swaying from side to side, ducking and rising to avoid blows, will surely leave him vulnerable and open in a spot which ordinarily he would safeguard. Both his left and right sides will be exposed. Then is the time to draw back your right or left, one to push the blows aside or to catch the impact of the blows on the forearm or on the glove and, with the other, either to hook to side of the body or uppercut to the jaw.

Swinging then is, of course, impossible. You are too close to him. Your hook or uppercut is the only punch to throw.

As a matter of fact, most fighters punch in spurts or flurries. No one could possibly continue at high speed through the length of a fight. Thus every flurry must come to an end, if only because of the natural caution of the experienced fighter. The only thing to do is to wait out a flurry, being careful to see that whatever spot is open is not a vital place.

Then watch for the opening, which must come--and let go.

The best "cover-up" is not the crossing of the arms in front of and slightly over the head. It is obvious that it would be a slightly awkward way of protecting the face and body, as it would leave little opportunity for a quick change to offense. Should you have your arms crossed and see an opening, in order to withdraw one arm from across or under the other, you could not help but telegraph your intention and, to any up-and-coming fighter, that would be more than sufficient warning that he has exposed himself, and then he would most likely "cover-up" himself.

The better way is to have your arms both extended in front of you, but in a sort of upward angle made by bending both elbows and lifting the forearms almost vertical. You must not extend the arms too far away from your chest. Coupled with this position of your arms, it will be best to crouch by bending your body forward slightly at the waist, your chin sunk almost on your chest, and one shoulder raised higher than the other.

COVERING-UP

In this way a blow directed at your chin may be parried by a flick of your left or right forearm, which would either be deflected to the right or left or punched down. If your opponent should by his blow, intended or landed, overstep himself—that is, be slightly off balance, or leave himself uncovered, you have either hand to let fly into his body or jaw.

FEINTING

The other day we had occasion to see one of these rustic dramas our Hollywood directors delight in bringing to the screen—a drama concocted of ninety percent "hokum" and ten percent pure unreality. With the story we cannot quarrel because this being a diverse world, there is a market for everything and each person is entitled to his taste in "pap."

However, what seemed funny not alone to ye editor but to most of the public was a "prize-fight" in which one of the fighters was heard to whisper to the other, "Your shoe's open." Then, of course, the other professor forgot that he was in a fight, bent over to look, and the "slicker" gave him the "haymaker."

We do not say that things like that could not happen in prize fights. There are some entrants in the ring who are not overburdened with gray matter that might be fooled by such an obvious trick. Guile of this type is childish and even the puerile mentality of some fighters could understand that.

It is not, however, necessary for any fighter to resort to that sort of antic. There is a legitimate way of putting an opponent off-guard, and it is known to all fighters as FEINTING.

To explain its meaning is to tell its action.

You merely start a blow, be it jab, hook or swing, being careful not to allow too much freedom of motion lest the momentum of the throw carry out the seeming intention of your blow and spoil the thing you are trying to carry out.

Then, just as it is about to land, halt its motion. Your opponent, if he knows his business, will throw out his forearm to ward off the blow.

He will either endeavor to push it to the right or left of him, or catch its impact on his wrist or glove. Since this was only a feint and never intended to really land, you have held your other hand loosely cocked close to your chest, and now that his glove has contacted yours and left himself open, you bore in with the other arm and fist, using either a hook or an uppercut, whichever is most available.

In this connection it is unwise to look directly at your opponent when you mean to feint him into an opening because oftentimes, as in the game of poker, your look will betray your intention. The experienced fighter looks at his opponent's feet. They tell him first of all whether the other is moving forward or backward, and sometimes the sudden tightening of the leg muscles will show that a forward spring is about to take place.

By looking clown at his feet also, while keeping corner of your eyes "peeled" to see any sign of relaxing of his guard, you direct his attention downward and often times he will involuntarily drop his arms, thinking you contemplate jabbing at his midsection.

This feinting is pure guile and seldom fools the fighter who has had many ring battles, because he is prepared with the same kind of ammunition and intends, if he can, to try it on you. Nevertheless, the true feint, that is, the blow that is actually thrown, although the action is subsequently arrested, may and often does fool any man. In any event it compels your opponent to make an effort to block your blow and that of necessity leaves him open. Since you planned that very thing, you are prepared if he is not.

THE RIGHT CROSS

As its name indicates. the right cross is a right-handed blow and yet, analyzing it, we must couple it with a left jab or swing. As a matter of fact, it would be more accurate to call it the "double-cross," because the combination of the two blows, left jab and right cross, are so used and in that order to deceive your opponent into preparing to defend himself against a left which at best would only be a light tap, while the right lands with telling force.

It is well noted at this point that practically without exception all seasoned veterans of the ring start an attack by leading with their lefts. The question one puts to himself is, why lead with the left? What is wrong with leading with the right?

The fact that everybody does it shouldn't of itself be an argument, except for the perfectly cogent reason that it is certain a left lead would have been abandoned long ago unless there was some actual advantage in its use. And there is.

Assume that you are a left-hander. Your natural pose would be, if you didn't know better, to take your stance with your right foot forward, your right arm extended and your left arm held against your chest. The vast majority of fighters are right handers. In opposing you they would stand with their left facing you, extended in front of them, left foot almost touching your right. Any right-handed blow you might throw could easily be warded off by their extended left arm; your left-handed blow would be so far away from their bodies that you would immediately telegraph to them that you intended to use it and that, too, would be parried without difficulty.

Thus, even natural left handers are taught to take a right-handed stance. viz.: to stand with the left foot extended in front, the left arm held bent at the elbow and slightly forward of the body, while the right arm is held close to the chest.

Since your opponent stands in the same position, neither your extended foot nor his will meet at any point, nor would your left arm meet his.

Now then, let's come down to the right cross.

Standing then in the natural right-hand pose, you step inward towards your opponent, lead with your left. We will give him credit for knowing how to avoid that blow. He will step to his left, which will be your right, and your blow will either graze his face slightly or miss him altogether. If you stopped there, you would have wasted a blow and left yourself open to a counter. But your intention was merely to make him think you were going to jab or swing your left at him and put him off-guard.

Immediately and with all the speed you can muster, you follow up with your cocked right, even while your left arm is still traveling toward him, and bring your right over your left arm in what we call the "right-cross" and sink it into his face, either on his cheek, or left side of his jaw.

The distance that right cross travels has added weight to it; the fact that you have thrown your left forward has naturally thrown your body forward and your head has been lowered with the motion, thus your whole body has followed both the left and the right blows and this has increased the force of the right blow tremendously.

The left lead has been an overhand one and has in this instance had but little, if any, effect, but your right-cross has been thrown in an upward arc and then a downward position, making almost a complete semi-circle. You will have landed your right blow in such a way as to have the knuckles land squarely on the cheek or jaw. It will have the effect of a mallet hitting against a stationary body.

LEFT LEAD

Should your opponent, in his effort to avoid your left jab, move forward to attempt some infighting, your right cross will then have even greater impact, for it will mean the meeting of two moving objects.

Those of us who attended the recent bout between Joe Louis and the Black Uhlan from Germany, Max Schmeling were treated to the spectacle of a great fighting machine being almost slaughtered by a continual flurry of right crosses.

The lithe Brown Bomber from Detroit had been taught to expect the usual cringing, quivering yellow-streaked fighter who was licked before he entered the ring. His reputation for annihilation cast such a shadow over all the challengers that they came into the ring with fear and trepidation, that Louis just shuffled over and "left-ed" them to death. He would stick out his long left arm and calmly proceed to cut and jab his opponent to ribbons, waiting until the combination of fear and suffering would hypnotize him into a semi-comatose state and then he would coldly apply his finishing, if not very merciful, knockout.

Schmeling didn't fear him. He didn't step back and out of harm's way. He fought it out. He waded in and time and time again he would lead with his left, have it pushed aside by Louis, and then bring over his right cross with ,such terrific force that each time the Detroit Death-Dealer found himself staggering and groggy.

The very last blow he received and which convinced him he had had enough was a crushing right cross flush against the left side of his jaw.

When the fight was over the entire left side of his face was swollen out of shape.

He could not seem to avoid those savage right crosses. He went down to defeat a victim of the universal error of not having perfected a good defense to a right cross.

RIGHT CROSS

K.O.!

ROLLING WITH THE PUNCH

Recklessness is a trait of the very young. But some fighters never grow up. In fact, only in rare instances and, with notable exceptions, those who "rushed in where angels fear to tread" had a short life in the ring and not a particularly merry one.

Ordinarily the fighter who takes five blows to land one makes a Roman holiday for the fickle crowds who want action and then some more action. The crafty warrior whose career is a steady upward climb discounts the plaudits of the crowd and, while giving the best that is in him, evades as many punches as he can, and the very fact that he succeeds in parrying most of the blows directed at him helps him maintain that calm, cool judgment required to best his opponent. A groggy boxer may have murder concealed in each fist, but he ends up by concealing that fact from both his opponent and the spectators and finds himself at last sniffing smelling-salts in the dressing room.

To few it is given to have that driving, ripping nervous energy that wipes out resistance and sets aside the skill and ability opposed, like some whirlwind or tornado sweeping everything in its path. "Terrible Terry" McGovern was one of those human explosives. Starting as a. bantam without any real knowledge of boxing, he tore through his class like a storm of locusts, destroying everyone that stood in his way. He blasted the featherweights and went on. And yet his career was a comparatively short one. He burned himself out before he knew it. Soon, a fresher, younger, more cautious fighter took his number and his title.

There's a lesson in it for those who have the eyes to see.

Who is not familiar with the fact there are two ways of catching a baseball? One is to stand perfectly still and let the ball hit your hand or even glove with its unspent force. This would eventually cause the hand to swell up and before long be incapacitated. The other is to "cushion" the blow. You will see, if you watch carefully, that the old timer will always catch the ball with a backward sweep of his glove so that instead of striking directly on a motionless object, it will strike, if at all, a moving object,—one that moves in the same direction as itself.

That may be done in boxing. It is called "rolling with the punch." It is usually possible to see the blow coming your way and, even if it be impossible to evade it entirely, its force may be lessened and made harmless by stepping backward or "fading" back in the direction the blow is traveling. When and if it lands, it will he just a grazing blow at best and will do no damage.

PASSING THE PUNCH

To the initiated this form of evading a punch is often known as "slipping the punch," but a more accurately descriptive phrase would be "passing the punch," because in essence, it is the movement to the left or right of the head and body to pass the punch, or to permit the blow to pass over the right or left shoulder.

When the fighters take their fighting poses, facing each other, as already noted, in most instances they will both stand with left arm slightly extended in front of them and their right arms held some short distance across their chests.

When the fighters take their fighting poses, facing each other, as already noted, in most instances they will both stand with left arm slightly extended in front of them and their right arms held some short distance across their chests.

One of them——the aggressor——will lead with his left, as he has been taught to do. The other will not, of course, step back if he sees the blow coming, for, if he did, he would place himself perhaps out of range of the punch, but would also lose the opportunity of retaliating.

He will either move a few inches, say about five or six, by shifting his body that distance to the right of that blow, in which ease the arm of his opponent would fall harmlessly over his left shoulder and then he could counter with his own left on the unprotected left side of the other; or he might step those same few inches to the left of that blow so that the other's arm would fall over his right shoulder, whereupon he would be able to bring up his own right fist either into the ribs of the aggressor or uppercut him by bringing his fist up in that upward arc until he reached his chin. Naturally he would have to use his left hand as a foil in order to ward off the possible attempt of the other to use his right, either punching the other's blow down or pushing them to the right or left.

It stands to reason that this passing the punch must be done with precision—that is, machine-like and measured timing—and withal speed, although no such ungainly haste that will cause the feet to trip or the body to lose balance. It would be wise to do that sidestepping to pass the punch with the heel and sole of both feet resting solidly on the ground so that no sudden change of pace or switch of direction on the part of your opponent will find you even slightly off-balance.

PASSING THE PUNCH

It must be obvious, even to a beginner. that it is riot always necessary to move the body to avoid a blow. For it is patent that to move the body, one must have more time and deliberation. Frequently an opponent will throw a punch which travels with such speed that nothing short of a miraculous coordination of mind and muscle makes it possible to even commence thought of moving the body. Then the time comes to merely move the head to one side. This requires quick thought and but little motion and is often the test of a good boxer. Economy of motion, a minimum of action, saves unnecessary strain on bone, flesh and nerves.

The easy "passing of the punch" by movement of the head to one side is disconcerting to your opponent in more ways than one. Not alone does he miss the mark, but he usually find himself propelled forward by the very force of his blow. If repeated it would soon develop in him the feeling that you cannot be reached. Nothing is so discouraging as a target that cannot be hit. If, in addition thereto, you are prepared to take advantage of the opening he leaves by his "miss," and counter to his unguarded body, with either or both of your hands, you may hurt him without fear df receiving a counter-attack.

PASSING LEFT JAB

DUCKING, BOBBING AND WEAVING

A fight crowd, the writer has found, is really a cross-section of the population of the locale of the contest. Therefore, it is made up of a diversity of elements, each with its own peculiar slant, likes and dislikes. Yet there is one thing each fan has in common with every other. His sympathy for the "under-dog." It is certainly this, rather than love of gore, that prompts the habitue of the fight arena to desire the fall of the current idol. The challenger usually goes into battle with the good wishes of the crowd.

The shorter fighter opposed to the long, lank, "string-bean" is one of those under-dogs beloved of a fan. He looks pitifully unequal to the task of repelling his taller opponent. And yet the shorter of the two has a decided advantage.

He may—and usually does duck the other's blows. While he cannot reach, let us say, the other's jaw or face, he can do terrible damage to the lankier man's mid-section, and it is here that repeated attacks may soften up the "bean-pole" so that he is soon whittled down to size.

Well, what does, "Ducking" mean? It shouldn't be necessary to answer such a question to the average boy in any American city of any size. If he never had an occasion to duck a punch in his youth, then he never had any youth.

The word itself indicates its meaning. Given sufficient time to see the blow coming your way, it is the simplest thing in the world to bend under the blow. Having bent below it, you have ducked it.

However, the ducking process is accompanied with a "bobbing" and "weaving."

Dempsey who was and still is the most famous exponent of this art, was accustomed to stand in opposition to his opponent in a crouch. He would bend his head forward, his body slightly slouched like a half-opened jack-knife, his knees partially bent and his arms so held against his chest as to permit his elbows to rest against his stomach, the fists pointing upward, while he swayed his whole body left, right, forward or backward. A blow thrown at him, would find him bending his knees a little more and his head under the blow. Often he would weave inside of his opponent's arms, ducking under them, get up close and then flat out with short rights and lefts, until the other contestant was a mass of red welts or lay prone on the ground.

BLOCKING PUNCH BY CATCHING OPPONENT'S BICEP

LONDON PRIZE RING RULES

If anyone remembers his youthful reading of that immortal work of Sir Walter Scott, "Ivanhoe" and can forget the "zeros" gathered from that hawk-eyed and vinegar-tongued teacher in high school over his or her failure to describe properly the tourneys and jousts pf medieval Merrie

England, there will come back to him the sweet flavor of antiquity which he must have felt when the master described these panoplied affairs of "honor."

It is indeed in that spirit and with the same feeling of 'reverence for the ancient, not with the idea of poking fun at the foibles of the sports man of that early time that we give below the essence of the London Prize Ring Rules. It will serve, as nothing else, perhaps, will to give an almost historic picture of the prize fighter of the pre-gaslight-era-days.

It will also convey to the careful reader the ludicrously desperate lengths to which the "bloods" of those days went to establish some spirit of fair play in the bosom of those early "plug—uglies."

For what they are worth, for better or worse, like them or not, without further ado, here are the London Prize Ring Rules:

(1) That the ring shall be made on turf. It shall be four and twenty feet square, formed of eight stakes and ropes, the latter extending in double lines, the uppermost line being four feet from the ground, and the lower, two feet from the ground. That in the center of the ring a mark be formed, to be termed the SCRATCH.

(2) That each man shall be attended to the ring by two seconds and a bottle-holder. That the combatants, on shaking hands, shall retire until the seconds of each have tossed for choice of position, which adjusted, the winner shall choose his corner according to the state of the wind or sun, and conduct his man thereto; the loser taking the opposite diagonal corner.

(3) That each man shall be provided with a handkerchief of a color suitable to his fancy, and that the seconds shall tie these handkerchiefs to the upper end of one of the center stakes. These handkerchiefs are to be known as "colors." The winner in the battle

shall be entitled to both handkerchiefs or colors. These shall be the trophy of victory.

(4) There shall be two umpires, to be chosen by the seconds or backers. These may take exception to any breach of the rules. A referee shall be chosen by the umpires, unless otherwise agreed upon. To him all disputes shall be referred. His decision shall be final and binding on all matters in dispute. The referee shall be provided with a watch for calling the time. The referee shall withhold all opinion until appealed to by the umpires.

(5) That the men shall be stripped upon entering the ring and the seconds shall examine their drawers; if any objection arises as to insertion of improper substances therein, they shall appeal to their umpires, who, with the concurrence of the referee, shall direct what alteration shall be made.

(6) That the spikes in the fighting boots (evidently shoes worn by fighters at that time bore spikes) shall he confined to three in number, which shall not exceed three-eighths of an inch from the sole oi the boot, and shall not be less than one-eighth of an inch broad at the point; two to he placed in the broadest part of the sole, and one in the heel; and that in the event of a man's wearing any other spikes, either in the toes or elsewhere, he shall be compelled either to remove them or provide other boots properly spiked. If he should refuse to do so, the penalty shall be the loss of the stakes.

(7) When ready, both men shall be conducted, each to that side of the scratch next his corner previously chosen, the seconds on the one side, and the men on the other. having shaken hands, the former shall immediately leave the ring, and there remain till the round be finished. and on no pretense whatever approach their principals during the round without permission from the referee. Penalty for disobedience to be the loss of the battle to the offending parties.

(8) That at the end of the round, when one or both of the men shall he down, the seconds shall step into the ring and carry or conduct their principal to his corner, there affording him the necessary assistance, and that no person whatever be permitted to interfere in this duty.

(9) That on the expiration of thirty seconds the referee shall cry "Time," upon which each man shall rise from the knee of his

second and walk to his own side of scratch unaided; the seconds immediately leaving the ring. The penalty for either of them remaining eight seconds after the call of "Time" to be the loss o[the battle to his principal, and that either man failing to be at scratch within eight seconds shall be deemed to have lost the battle.

(10) That no person, except the seconds or the referee, shall be permitted to enter the ring during the battle, nor till it shall have been concluded; that in the event of such unfair practice, or the ropes or stakes being disturbed or removed, it shall be in the power of the referee to award the victory to that man who, in his honest opinion, shall have the best of the contest.

(11) That the seconds shall not interfere, advise or direct the adversary of their principal, and shall refrain from all offensive expressions, (evidently there were no lack of "Bronx Cheers" or their equivalent even in those days), in all respects conducting themselves with order and decorum, and confine themselves to the diligent and careful discharge of their duties to their principals.

(12) In picking up their own men, if the seconds willfully injure the antagonist of their principal, the latter shall be deemed to have forfeited the battle on the decision of the referee.

(13) That it shall be a fair "stand-up fight." If either man shall willfully throw himself down without receiving a blow, whether blows shall have previously been exchanged or not, he shall be deemed to have lost the battle. (There seems to have been "floppers" then too.) This rule, however, shall not apply to a man who in a close slips down from the grasp of his opponent to avoid punishment, or from obvious accident or weakness.

(14) That butting with the head shall be deemed foul, and the party resorting to this practice shall be deemed to have lost the battle.

(15) A blow struck when a man is thrown or down shall deemed foul. A man with one knee and one hand on the or with both knees on the ground, shall be deemed down; and a blow given in either of these position shall be considered foul, providing always that, when in such position, the man so down shall not himself strike or attempt to strike.

(16) That a blow struck below the waistband shall be deemed foul, and that, in a close, seizing an antagonist below the waist, by the thigh, or otherwise, shall be deemed foul. (The reader will note that the word "waistband" was used advisedly then, because most of the fighters were so barrel-girthed that a waist without a "band" could not be distinguished at all.)

(17) That all attempts to inflict injury by gouging, or tearing the flesh with the fingers or nails, and biting, shall be deemed foul. (That will give you a picture of what took place in fights prior to the establishing of these rules—-and perhaps a good deal after that.)

(18) Kicking, or deliberately falling on an antagonist with the knees or otherwise when down, shall be deemed foul.

(19) All bets shall be paid as the battle money after a fight is awarded.

(20) The referee and umpires shall take their positions in front of the center stake, outside the ropes.

(21) Due notice shall be given by the stakeholder, of the day and place where the battle money is to be given up, and that he be exonerated from all responsibility upon obeying the direction of the referee; all parties are strictly bound by these rules; that in future all articles of agreement for a contest be entered into with a strict and willing adherence to the letter and spirit of these rules.

(22) That in the event of magisterial or other interference, (can't you see just how law-abiding these prize-fights were at that time?), or in case of darkness coming on, the referee shall have the power to name the time and place for the next meeting, if possible on the same day, or as soon thereafter as may be. (It was not at all unusual for fighters, seconds, referee and the crowds to have to go to three or four different places in one day with the minions of the law just one jump behind them—in order to see a fight or the continuation of one.) In naming the second or third place, the nearest spot shall be selected to the original place of fighting where there is a chance of its being fought out.

(23) That if the fight is not decided on the day. all bets shall be withdrawn, unless the fight shall be resumed the same week, between Sunday and Sunday, in which case the referee's duties shall continue, and the bets stand and shall be decided by the

event. The battle money shall remain in the hands of the stake holder until fairly won or lost by a fight, unless a draw be mutually agreed upon, or, in ease of postponement, one of the principals shall be present, when the man in the ring shall be awarded the stakes.

(24) Any pugilist voluntarily quitting the ring, previous to the deliberate judgment of the referee being obtained, shall be deemed to have lost the fight.

(25) That on an objection being made by the second or umpire the men shall retire to their corners, and there remain until the decision of the appointed authorities shall be obtained; that if pronounced "out," the battle shall be at an end but if "fair," "time" shall be called by the party appointed, and the man absent from scratch in eight seconds after shall be deemed to have lost the fight. The decision in all cases to be given promptly and irrevocably, for which purpose the umpires and the referee should be invariably close together.

(26) That if a man leaves the ring, either to escape punishment or for any other purpose, without the permission of the referee, unless he is involuntarily forced out, shall forfeit the battle.

(27) That the use of hard substances, such as stones, or sticks, or of resin in the hand, during the battle, shall be deemed foul, and that on the requisition of the seconds of either man the accused shall open his hands for the examination of the referee.

(23) That hugging on the ropes shall be deemed foul. That a man held by the neck against the stakes, or upon or against ropes, shall be considered down, and all interference with him in that position shall be tool. That if a man in any way makes use of the ropes or stakes to aid in squeezing his adversary he shall be deemed the loser of the battle; that if a man m a close embrace reaches the ground with his knees, his adversary shall immediately loose him or lose the battle.

CHRONOLOGICALLY SPEAKING

The evolution of the "Game," for after all, it is that, even if at times it had and has its aspects of brutality and an element of the mercenary, centered largely around the "big boys" or the heavyweights.

Essentially, prizefighting was a strong man's pastime. From its infancy the sport called for qualities of the body, though little of mind, and it earned its popularity because of universal love of bodily prowess. For some reason, not particularly hard to fathom, hand-to-hand combat had little fascination for the better classes of society in Anglo-Saxon countries, and thus for a long time it was a social outcast and pariah in England and in America.

In its earliest days it was a pleasantly diverting sport for the betting fraternity in old England—that class of young scions of nobility and the landed gentry whose leisure hours were given over to play and whose ordinary effeminate dress and speech affectations were leavened by the glow of manly virility which being patrons of the "science of boxing" lent them.

It was, therefore, no less a personage than the Duke of Cumberland who set himself up as a patron of the "pugs." His special protege was one John Broughton. This worthy, having the backing of that noble though rather unsportsmanlike figure, went in big for teaching the "art and science" to the upper classes. In 1747 from his home in Haymarket, London, he issued such illuminating announcements as these (speaking of himself)

" *will give instruction in the 'mystery' of boxing; blows. cross-buttocks. Persons of quality and distinction may not be barred from these lectures.*

Mufflers will be provided to secure them against black eyes, broken jaws and bloody noses."

Of course .he wasn't just a "professor" of boxing. He was also, as he styled himself, "Champion of England," undoubtedly by virtue of the fact that there were very few at that time that knew anything about boxing or cared to argue the point.

In 1750, due to his patron's desire to "Clean up" some money, he was matched with another bruiser by the name of Jack Slack, a butcher. As far as Broughton was concerned, Slack might just as well have been a black-smith, for when they met the first thing Slack did was to let fly a sledge-hammer fist, hitting Broughton right between the eyes and blinding him. Science or no science the master could not very well fight without being able to see his opponents, so he went down ingloriously to defeat.

The Duke of Cumberland, a sterling sportsman, having lost his stakes, cursed his protege out in the best King's English, abandoned this first love, and spent the rest of his days philandering, a sport which might cost more but which brought more soul satisfying results. Needless to say boxing had trouble recovering from this black eye and for a long time it remained in disrepute.

Strangely enough boxing in America found its first exponents among negroes in the South. And yet not so-strangely, for most young men of the landed aristocracy of Dixie thought their educations incomplete unless they spent a portion of their time in England and other capitols of Europe. Accordingly they imbibed the same ideas of sport that their English prototypes held. Since it would have been demeaning for them to engage in battle themselves. they trained their slaves or at least, the strongest of them to box in order to amuse themselves at the spectacles presented.

In 1810, a freed slave. Tom Molyneux, sometimes called the "Moore" held the center of the boxing spotlight. He cut wide swathes among the fighting men, but his opponents were all other "gentlemen of color." It was not yet respectable for white men to engage in a lowering sport. It was not until 1316 that the lordly white skin in America found it something he could touch without holding his nose.

The first man in the United States to bring some glory to the "game" was that sturdy Boston Strong Boy John L. Sullivan. He had been a wrestler of parts and a circus strong man. It was no great effort for him to bring ham-like fists into the squared circle. His efforts decimated the crop of fighters of his day like a giant reaping machine. It was only in the latter part of his career that he bowed to some sort of science and became the protagonist of the gloved fist. He had always fought with bare knuckles. Everyone else did.

It was told that his blows were so powerful that once when in a rage—and he was often in a bellowing tantrum—he struck an iron stanchion with his bare fist and the iron bent under the blow. We cannot present any affidavits under oath as to the truth of this story. It is enough that the story is told to know that he was a mighty man.

For ten years the almost legendary strong boy held the championship. He gave it to youth, a cleaner liver and one who eschewed the owing howl. James J. Corbett, [Gentleman Jim] was the first one to use nothing but the five-ounce glove. A trim, slender well-built, scientific athlete, who took his fighting seriously, found the measure of the old master and, with the combined help of his own skill and the ravage of whiskey on Sullivan tore the slightly tarnished crown from the latter's head.

Yet Corbett too, went the way of all flesh. Soon a faster, harder fighter made him step down. "Ruby Robert" was coming along, Robert Fitzsimmons an Australian freak--only in the sense that he was far from being an Adonis. He was lank, ungainly and had big, brown freckles over almost the whole of his body. A bald head with a brain that was worthy of better things helped him outsmart and outfight his antagonists.

On March 17, 1897, Fitzsimmons made history with his famous "Solar Plexus" punch. Of course he didn't name it that. He didn't even know that he had used it. But the newspaper men who saw the fight noted the way that corded right fist of his sank into the region to the right of Corbett's heart where the diaphragm begins. Jim went down, Ruby Bob helped him along with a light left to the jaw, which added nothing more to the already comatose champion—who was then no more.

Two years later a young boiler maker who had been Corbett's sparring partner, was on the way up. Old Fitz was then forty years old, far too gone in ring years to hope to have any further longevity. On that notable day, June 9, 1899, in world renowned Coney Island Fitz went down after a marvelous fight in which he almost had young Jeffries down a number of times.

In the eleventh round, as a well-known sports writer then described it, "Fitz landed a right to the ear. Jeffries countered with a right under the heart. By then Fitz was desperate. He left himself wide open, walking toward Jim, gambling on a chance swing to land a knock-out. He took a hard left jab on the chin and swung his own left for the button. It landed but Jeffries beat him to it with a full arm left which landed squarely on Bob's chin. Fitz dropped his hands, swayed on his feet. Instantly Jim was upon him. He sent another left hand on the chin which shot Fitz's head back with a snap. Then Jim brought up a terrific right swing which landed on the point of the chin. Fitz crumbled to the floor, out like a light. It took ten minutes to revive him."

Thus passed the most colorful fighter of all times. He fought a number of fights after that, but they were anti-climactic. Thereafter he was just another fighter.

Then came a large black cloud across the boxing moon. There arose in Gotham a colored giant, a good-natured, grinning, gold-toothed negro who was young, lusty and ambitious. And again youth took its toll.

On July 4, 1910, in the broiling sun, the two gladiators faced each other—the black and the white. One, a little tired of it all, the other eager and willing.

Jeffries was then a prosperous land-owner, seeking to retire to the ease of his inn. The other a roistering, black blade, still poor enough to have the proper incentive. In the 15th round, Johnson uncorked one of those abnormally long arms of his—his left—snaked it straight across and into James J.'s jaw hitting him right on the point of it, knocking him to the resin and the rest he had sought.

Soon the newspaper men were talking of this "White Hope' and that it became the duty of some white man to beat this black interloper. Many tried, but Johnson, with monotonous regularity disposed of the various "hopes" and soon became the "White Man's Burden."

But it's a long lane that has no turning. The trail of dissipation and revelry led at last to Johnson's Golgotha. A real White Hope sprang up at last-Jess Willard. He weighed only 240 pounds, and was well over six feet four. A behemoth. a mastodon. In Havana. on July 5, 1915, when the rest of the world was at war, Willard made his bid for the abdication of the colored champion. Maybe Willard was the great fighter some thought him. Maybe he was better than Johnson on that day. It is our private thought that Johnson fought two men in the ring in Havana-Willard and himself. He had made himself into a shadow of what he had been. High living laid him low. With the aid of the thorough fists of Willard he sank to the canvas a, sadder if not a wiser man.

And now we approach our next royalty with hated breath. William Harrison Dempsey, the California boy, known and loved as Jack Dempsey still holds the center of this writer's-heart as the one fighter who lent color to the game, lifted it into world renown and left it with its luster undimmed and untarnished.

Of his rapid rise most of us are aware. He was 190 lbs. of fused and capped dynamite when he met fess Willard at Toledo on July 4, 1919. From the moment he entered the ring, it was like some feral creature let out of a cage. He raged and tore into the man mountain that opposed him, unaware of the other's awesome reputation or his gargantuan size. He ripped and slashed jess into ribbons. He was avenging wraithe to the tormented pachyderm. Jess Willard couldn't touch him—couldn't see him. Before the astonished eyes of the wildly clamoring mob, he lowered the 240 lbs. of beef and brawn that was Willard to the floor.

He wasn't the only one who had licked Willard. The "Wild Bull of the Pampas," the Argentinian, Luis Angel Firpo had done the trick after him. So that Jack couldn't refuse him the honor of trying to repeat the process on him.

On September 14, 1923, Firpo met Dempsey. Firpo was well named the "Wild Bull of the Pampas.' He had little if any knowledge of boxing, but he rushed like a wild bull few had been able to withstand him. He knew no fear and seemed to feel no pain.

After meeting the floor of the ring over and over again he got up, rushed at Jack and with a blow that was more than half a push propelled his lighter opponent across the ring and out of the ropes into the laps of the scribes of the press. In the excitement the referee forgot to count. There is no doubt that Jack got more than a "break" from the official. He must have been out of the ring for more than twenty counts, although the actual count after he got back into the ring with the assistance of the newspapermen was less than ten.

Returning to the ring he was Hell let loose. He ripped and tore at the other's vitals again. Firpo was compelled to clinch and hold. Out of one of those holding bouts, Dempsey tore free, sent over a powerful left to the chin, followed It by a destructive right directly on the button—and good-bye Firpo.

Our friend jack Dempsey is now a wealthy restaurateur, somewhat of a bon vivant and a person beloved by his fellow New Yorkers. He acts as referee himself at times.

But he, too, had to experience, the heart-break that comes with the loss of the title.

There was a Marine. A clean-cut, if colorless, American lad who was methodical, studious and a scientific boxer. Never theretofore known to have a lethal blow in either of his fists. Yet James J. Tunney, known as Gene Tunney, did the trick no one else had ever been able to do, won from the great Dempsey twice by decision.

Gene was called a synthetic fighter, one who was built up carefully. Not a natural. Yet withal he exhibited rare courage, fine sportsmanship and admirable stick-to-it-iveness. He was different from most of the fighters of all times. Like Corbett, he was a gentleman and like him was proud of having read more than one book.

Having won fame and fortune, he retired to live the life of a cultured gentleman, leaving the ring before he could be defeated by some aspiring youngster. He left behind him a tradition of cleanliness of body and mind and is still an inspiration to the rest of American youth. He will not, perhaps, remain the idol of the pug or the plug-ugly who respects only roughness and toughness, but he will always be remembered by those who love the game for its spirit of fair play and for the chance it gives some penniless youngster to rise out of his sordid surroundings to a life of usefulness and leisure to improve one's position in life.

There followed his short reign, such men as Sharkey, Camera, Baer, Schmeling and Braddock, but aside from the up-and-coming Louis, the Brown Bomber from Detroit, their lives hold no particular highlights of an historical value. Long before their day the Million Dollar Gate was established and the spectacles of championship fights are no longer the novelty they used to be. Radio has made them common-place in every home, and the rapid shift of fortune of the heavy-weights holds, only passing interest.

We know that the champion of today may be the "bum" of tomorrow. We know also that most of those that leave the ring today, whether of their own volition or by the knock-out route usually end in comfortable middle-age, wealthy and respected. The stalwarts of the past still engage our bemused eyes and it is to them that we turn tor entertaining anecdote and instruction.

The heavyweights are by no means the only fighter worth having seen or to be seen. There have been sterling athletes in the bantam, feather, lightweight, middleweight and light-heavyweight classes. Some of them have been colorful. Some of them have fought with science amounting almost to genius. Yet our first love has been and probably will always be like the big cats in the circus, the **HEAVYWEIGHTS**.

STANCE

BLOCKING LEFT JAB

LEFT HOOK TO BODY-

-AND OUT!